PANZERS IN NORTH-WEST EUROPE

For details of this picture see page 49.

BRUCE QUARRIE
PANZERS IN NORTH-WEST EUROPE

WORLD WAR 2 PHOTO ALBUM NUMBER 5

A selection of German wartime photographs from the Bundesarchiv, Koblenz

PSL Patrick Stephens, Cambridge

© Patrick Stephens Limited 1979

All rights reserved. No part of this publication may be reproduced, stored in a retrieval system or transmitted, in any form or by any means, electronic, mechanical, photocopying, recording or otherwise, without prior permission in writing from Patrick Stephens Limited. Duplicates of photographs in this book may be obtained for reproduction purposes only from the Bundesarchiv, Koblenz.

First published in 1979

British Library Cataloguing in Publication Data

World War 2 photo album.
   5: Panzers in North-West Europe.
   1. World War, 1939-1945 — Pictorial works I.
Quarrie, Bruce
940.53′022′2   D743.2

ISBN 0 85059 342 5 (casebound)
ISBN 0 85059 322 0 (softbound)

Photoset in 10pt Plantin Roman. Printed in Great Britain on 100 gsm Pedigree coated cartridge and bound by The Garden City Press Limited, Letchworth, Hertfordshire, SG6 1JS, for the publishers, Patrick Stephens Limited, Bar Hill, Cambridge, CB3 8EL.

CONTENTS

CAMPAIGN MAP 6
AUTHOR'S INTRODUCTION 7
ABOUT THE PHOTOGRAPHS 12
THE PHOTOGRAPHS 13
APPENDICES 93

Acknowledgements
The author and publisher would like to express their sincere thanks to Dr Matthias Haupt and Herr Meinrad Nilges of the Bundesarchiv for their assistance, without which this book would have been impossible.

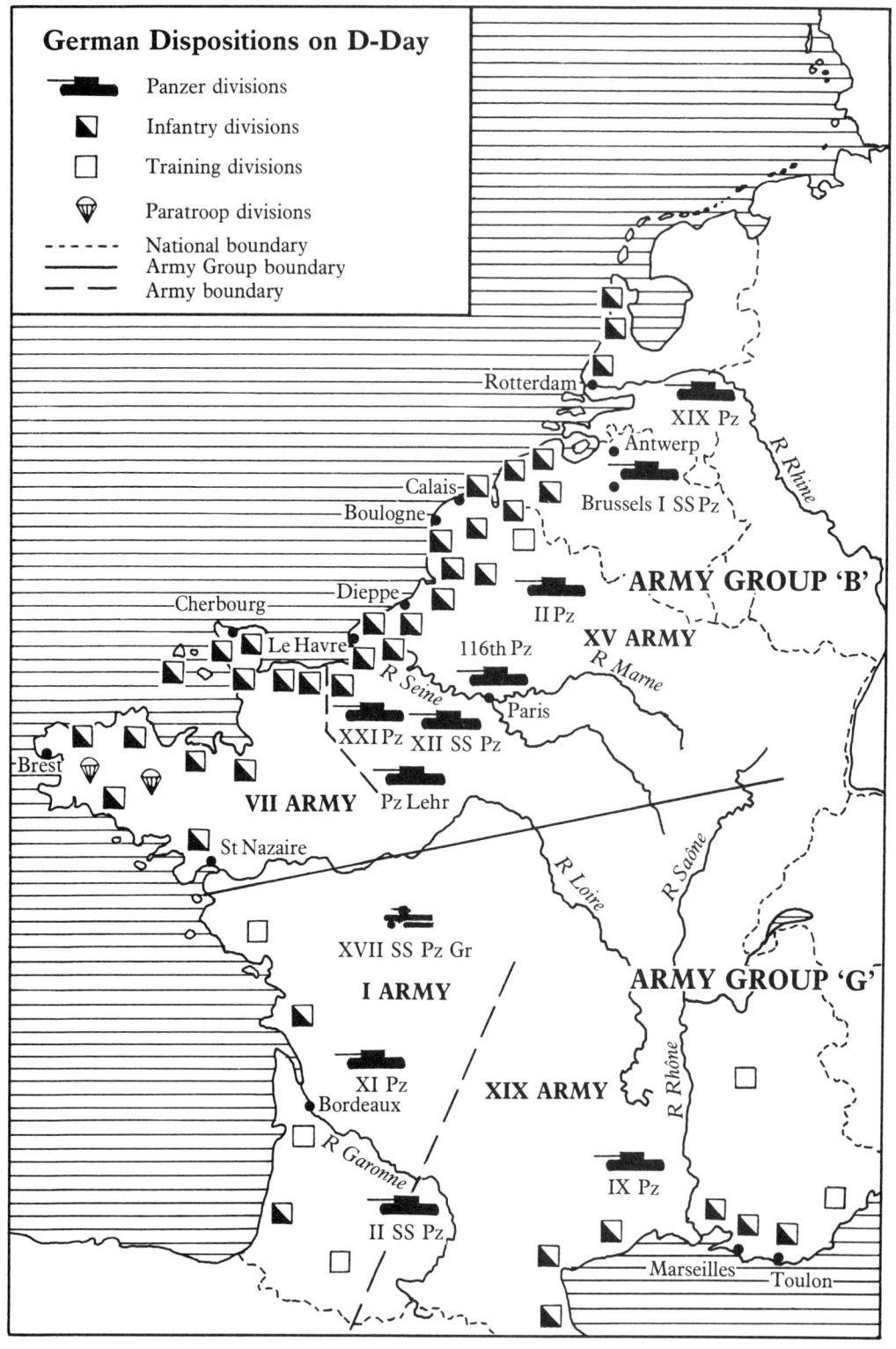

Total confusion reigned in Berlin and Paris. It was just after daybreak on June 6 1944, and preliminary reports of a massive Allied amphibious assault on the Normandy beaches near Caen were being received with incredulity. The Allies were supposed to open their long-expected second front in the Pas de Calais, not in Normandy! There, the vaunted Atlantic Wall scarcely existed in more than name. True, there were the rows of underwater obstacles designed to rip the bottoms from landing craft; true, there were fairly extensive minefields. But behind these there was a relatively empty shell.

Thanks to Allied deception measures and ultra-tight security around the ports and concentration areas in southern England, the German high command (OKW) remained firmly convinced that the Allied invasion was destined for the Pas de Calais region, where the Channel was narrowest. Moreover, the weather was surely too bad for a full-scale invasion? The landings in Normandy must, therefore, be a feint.

Thus the Germans lost vital hours and, as it turned out, days, during which the Allied hold on mainland Europe was precarious to say the least, and during which a concerted counter-attack by the available Panzer divisions could perhaps have thrown them back.

In June 1944 the Germans could muster a total of ten Panzer divisions in France. Closest to the beach-heads were three élite formations: the 21st Panzer Division under Generalmajor Feuchtinger, the Panzer 'Lehr' Division under Fritz Bayerlein, and the 12th SS Panzer Division 'Hitler Jugend' under Oberführer Fritz Witt. These three formations, together with the 116th Panzer Division outside Rouen and the 2nd Panzer Division slightly to its north, fell under command of the 15th Army. The 7th Army, whose responsibility included the Normandy beaches, had no Panzer divisions under command.

Further north, the 1st SS Panzer Division Leibstandarte 'Adolf Hitler' was based near Brussels, and the 19th Panzer Division was located in Holland. To the south were the 9th and 11th Panzer Divisions and the 2nd SS Panzer Division 'Das Reich' (see Appendix 1 for Orders of Battle and locations). Due to Allied aerial supremacy, moving these divisions to the threatened sector was to prove a hazardous and costly undertaking since – although the effects of Allied fighter-bomber attacks on German *tanks* have usually been exaggerated – the necessarily large 'tails' of support vehicles were very vulnerable.

The Germans had other problems too. Rommel, commander of Army Group B, was at home on leave, and von Rundstedt, overall commander of German forces in the west, had to clear movement orders for his three most rapidly available Panzer divisions with Berlin. Thus, although the Allied landings were hardly unopposed – the Americans, without any amphibious tanks, suffering particularly heavily on Omaha beach – the German counter-attack was delayed to such an extent that, when it finally occurred, it was too late.

The countryside upon which the invasion fell was not ideal tank country apart from a relatively flat and open area around and to the south of Caen. For the most part, the remainder consisted of close *bocage* – a region of small fields with narrow sunken lanes and thick hedgerows. In this type of terrain the Germans, with their superior weapons, lost their tactical advantage over the relatively lightly armed British and American tanks – Shermans, Cromwells and Churchills for the most part.

The mainstay of the German Panzer divisions by 1944 was the PzKpfw V Panther tank. The Panther was a MAN design which had been accepted in September 1942. It was closely based in many respects on the Soviet T-34 which had greatly impressed German troops fighting on the Eastern Front, and featured similarly well-sloped armour plates. These were in direct contrast to the plates on other German tanks – the PzKpfw III, PzKpfw IV and Tiger – which consisted largely of flat, vertical or near-vertical surfaces. The advantage of sloped armour is that it tends to deflect armour-piercing shot and thus gives greater protection for a given armour thickness.

The Panther had frontal armour 80 mm thick sloped at an angle of 35 degrees from the vertical, and 40 mm thick sloped at angles of between 50 and 90 degrees on its hull sides and rear. Its turret front was a formidable 110 mm thick (120 mm on the mantlet) sloped at 80 degrees from the vertical, while the turret sides were 45 mm thick at an angle of between 62 and 65 degrees. The weakest points, as on all tanks, were the roof and the floor, a mere 15 to 20 mm thick, making it vulnerable to mines and attack from the air. Against ground opponents, however, its frontal armour was relatively impervious except at point-blank range.

The Panther was powered by a 700 hp Maybach 12-cylinder engine which could drive it at up to 46 km/h (29 mph) on the road, 24 km/h (15 mph) cross-country. Its 730 litres (160 gallons) of fuel gave it a range of 177 km (110 miles). It was crewed by five men (commander, driver, hull machine-gunner/radio operator, gunner and loader) and weighed 44·8 tons.

For armament, the Panther carried the formidable 7·5 cm KwK 42 L/70 high-velocity anti-tank gun which had a muzzle velocity of up to 1,120 metres per second (3,675 fps) depending on the type of round being used. Eighty-two rounds of ammunition were carried for this weapon in addition to over 4,000 rounds for its two 7·92 mm machine-guns.

Alongside the Panther, the most numerous German tank was the veteran PzKpfw IV, a Krupp design which had been progressively up-armoured and up-gunned since its introduction in 1937. By 1944 the most common variant in use was the Ausf (Mark) H. Weighing in at 25 tons, this vehicle was powered by a 300 hp Maybach 12-cylinder engine giving it a top speed of 40 km/h (25 mph) and a range of 200 km (125 miles). Compared with the Panther, it had very thin armour protection – maximum 50 mm – and that hardly sloped at all from the vertical. To give it extra protection against Allied hollow-charge anti-tank projectiles, the PzKpfw IVH was usually fitted with additional 'spaced' armour around its turret and hull sides. The concept behind this was that a hollow-charge missile would explode itself harmlessly in the space between the side-skirts and the main armour of the tank.

The PzKpfw IVH was also armed with a 7·5 cm gun, the KwK 40, but this was shorter-barrelled than the Panther's KwK 42 (L/48 compared with L/70) and consequently had a lower muzzle velocity (990 m/s or 3,248 fps). Muzzle velocity was crucial in determining the effectiveness of a tank gun when firing solid shot, and gave extra range with hollow-charge projectiles. Eighty-seven rounds were carried for the main gun and over 3,000 rounds of machine-gun ammunition.

Although outclassed by 1944, the PzKpfw IV was still a most useful tank which could take on Shermans or Cromwells at roughly equal odds.

The third major type of German tank in use in 1944 was the PzKpfw VI Tiger I, a formidable heavy AFV weighing no less than 55 tons.

The result of a design competition between Porche and Henschel, which the latter won, the Tiger had first entered service in 1941 on the Russian front and had originally been encountered by the Anglo-Americans in Tunisia (see *World War 2 Photo Album 1: Panzers in the Desert*). It was also powered by a 12-cylinder Maybach engine producing 700 hp, but due to its extreme weight could only travel at 38 km/h (24 mph).

What made it so formidable was a combination of two factors – extremely thick armour plate and a potent 8·8 cm gun. The Tiger I's frontal armour was 100 mm thick (110 on the mantlet) and still as high as 80–82 mm around the stern, upper hull and turret sides. This made it virtually invulnerable to Allied anti-tank guns, although its low manoeuvrability meant that it could be outflanked and disabled by firing at its tracks and road wheels. However, when possible, Tiger commanders tried to avoid this by standing off and using the superior range of their 8·8 cm guns to hold off the lighter British and American tanks.

The 8·8 cm gun was a modified version of the famous 8·8 cm anti-aircraft gun, designated KwK 36 L/56. This had a lower muzzle velocity than the 7·5 cm weapons fitted to the PzKpfw IV or Panther, but the extra shell weight made up for a great deal. Ninety-two rounds of ammunition were carried plus nearly 4,000 rounds for the hull and turret machine-guns. Like the PzKpfw IV and Panther, the Tiger was crewed by five men.

The last major tank type encountered by the Allies in North-West Europe, albeit in small numbers, was the Tiger II or 'King Tiger'. The first production models of this monster had begun appearing at the beginning of 1944. Once again, it was the result of a design competition between Porsche and Henschel which the latter won, although some 50 Porsche-type turrets were fitted to Tiger IIs.

At the time of its appearance the Tiger II was the heaviest, best armed and most thickly armoured tank in the world. Moreover, its design had been strongly influenced by the success of the Panther and, apart from sheer size, the two vehicles were very similar in appearance. Weighing 69·7 tons and crewed, again, by five men, the Tiger II was grossly underpowered, having, in fact, the same 12-cylinder, 700 hp, HL 230 P 30 engine as the Panther, which was some 25 tons lighter! Not surprisingly, this gave it poor manoeuvrability, a high rate of mechanical breakdown, and a top speed of a mere 17 km/h (10·6 mph) cross-country.

However, as a defensive weapon it was a superb vehicle. Not only did it have well-sloped armour of up to 185 mm thickness (mantlet), but it also mounted the long-barrelled 8·8 cm KwK 43 L/71 anti-tank gun which had a muzzle velocity of 1,130 m/s (3,707 fps). Eighty-four rounds of ammunition were carried for this weapon.

Most German tanks at this time were liberally covered with a type of cement paste known as zimmerit, an anti-magnetic compound which prevented hollow-charge magnetic mines being attached to the vehicles. This gave them a rough, ridged appearance as can be seen in many of the photos.

The majority of German tanks by this period of the war were painted a uniform dark yellow over which mottle camouflage in brown, green and/or grey could be applied by individual crews. National and tactical markings also tended to be smaller than earlier in the war, and divisional insignia were conspicuous by their absence on the majority of Panthers and Tiger IIs (although they still proliferated on the older vehicles). Individual names, such as girlfriends', appear to have been a special feature of several 'Hitler Jugend' vehicles.

'Hitler Jugend' crews also revelled in wearing a unique 'uniform' – ex-U-boat crew black leather jackets and trousers. These are visible in some of the photographs and appear to have been issued to (commandeered by?) 'Hitler Jugend' personnel exclusively. Other SS tank crews in this theatre wore the standard SS-pattern short, double-breasted black Panzer jacket and trousers, or one- or two-piece mottle camouflaged overalls. Army tank crews normally wore plain black overalls ('boiler suits') or the standard black Panzer uniform.

Self-propelled gun crews sometimes wore the above, especially when crewed by Panzer regiment personnel, but were more usually garbed in the field-grey equivalent with artillery red instead of Panzer pink Waffenfarbe.

Returning from technical matters to the campaign itself, the first German counter-measures were taken by the 21st and 'Lehr' Panzer Divisions, which moved up piecemeal during daylight, were mercilessly hammered from the air, and proved unable to make significant headway.

The Americans were the first to make any major progress, heading westwards through the *bocage* towards the vital port of Cherbourg. On the other flank, however, Montgomery was initially unable to make any headway at all against the stubborn German Panzers. 21st Panzer Division spoiled an attack around the west of Caen while the British 7th Armoured Division ran into a packet of trouble from Tiger Is of the 501st Heavy Tank Battalion, Leibstandarte 'Adolf Hitler', commanded by Germany's leading tank 'ace', Obersturmführer Michael Wittman.

Wittman (see photos), with a mere five tanks, succeeded in knocking out no fewer than 25 Cromwells of the 22nd Armoured Brigade from a total force of 60, forcing Montgomery's advance to pull back in confusion. (For a more detailed account of this engagement, see my book *Tank Battles in Miniature 3: A wargamers' guide to the North-West European Campaign 1944-1945*, also published by Patrick Stephens Limited.)

A second attack in the Caen sector a few days later was also foiled, this time by the newly arrived 2nd SS Panzer Division 'Das Reich' reinforced by the 9th SS Panzer Division 'Hohenstaufen' and the 10th SS Panzer Division 'Frundsberg' which had been hastily transferred to Normandy from Poland.

But that was really the last German success. In the west, the Americans had encountered fierce resistance around St Lô which would hold them up until mid-July 1944, but shortly after the beginning of the month Montgomery's third attempt to break out of

Caen, Operation 'Goodwood', finally succeeded in breaking the German defence.

When St Lô eventually fell it also opened the floodgates for the Americans, and Patton's 3rd Army managed to break out, opening the route to Brittany and threatening to outflank German forces west and south of Paris. The British and American armoured pincers turned towards each other in an attempt to cut off the rapidly withdrawing German forces in what has become known as the 'Falaise Pocket', and succeeded in practically destroying 'Sepp' Dietrich's 5th Panzer Army, although due credit must go to the tough troops of SS 'Das Reich' who held open the neck of the pocket for four vital days during which a large number of men and vehicles managed to escape.

Paris fell on August 24 and the Germans were everywhere in retreat, falling back on the West Wall – a defensive zone along the German border up to 5 km deep and festooned with anti-tank obstacles, pillboxes, bunkers and minefields.

Montgomery devised an audacious, albeit ill-fated, scheme to break this line, dropping American and British paratroopers and glider-borne troops to take the three vital bridges at Eindhoven, Nijmegen and Arnhem to create an open road into the German rear for Horrocks' XXX Corps. Tragically, Allied intelligence had missed the presence of Wilhelm Bittrich's 9th and 10th SS Panzer Divisions in the vicinity and, although the Americans succeeded in capturing and holding the first two objectives, the British and Polish troops at Arnhem were defeated in one of the epic battles of all time before Horrocks could push through to relieve them.

The Allied onslaught slowed, partly at least due to supply problems, and the German defenders took the opportunity to regroup and rethink. Now, Hitler devised a scheme to rival the Arnhem operation in audacity, although it, too, was doomed to failure. This was a massive counter-offensive in the area where the Allies, it was hoped, would least expect it – through the mountainous and thickly forested Ardennes, where the German Panzers had originally swept forward to victory in 1940.

It is unfortunate that the Bundesarchiv files do not contain material from this epic encounter, as explained in the following notes about the photographs, for this would certainly prove fertile ground for the assiduous researcher. If any German citizen, perhaps a member or descendant of a member of Dietrich's 6th Panzer Army or Manteuffel's 5th Panzer Army, has such material, then I would welcome hearing from them and a new chapter could, perhaps, be written in the disjointed and usually biased annals of World War 2 heroism. As it is, in this book I am unable to give pictorial evidence from German sources as to the nature and quality of the fighting (one could go to the Imperial War Museum or US National Archives, but this would be to destroy the point of the series, which is to present the war pictorially from the German viewpoint).

Be that as it may, the course and outcome of the 'Battle of the Bulge', as it has become widely known, were in many ways a foregone conclusion; although German intelligence placed a great deal of reliance on Patton's sense of independence and frustration at being asked to pull someone else's chestnuts from the fire, they neglected the man's overriding sense of duty.

The German attack began well and swept all before it (not that there was a great deal). Bastogne was merely invested, however, when it should have been overwhelmed and, although German troops made significant headway, particularly in the south-west of the offensive thanks to the bad weather which kept Allied aircraft grounded, the Allied response was so swift that the offensive soon ground to a grudging halt, when the 2nd SS Panzer Division 'Das Reich' was on the point of re-crossing the River Meuse (Maas).

The main crisis arrived on December 21/22 1944, just before Christmas, The weather turned freezing cold and, apart from isolated units, there were no Allied units between the Germans and the river. Fortunately for the Allies, two Panzer divisions ran out of fuel, delaying their advance and, the following day, the weather cleared, allowing the fighter-bombers to take to the skies again. On Boxing Day Patton broke the Bastogne blockade and, shortly afterwards, the harried German Panzer commanders found themselves being assaulted with demands from Hitler for units to contain the latest Soviet winter offensive in the east. Many German soldiers made this pilgrimage and few returned to tell the tale since Stalin's labour camps excelled those of the Nazis.

Meanwhile, a renewed Anglo-American

offensive in the west ran into trouble, both from the weather and from unexpectedly tough German opposition. In fact, it was not until March 7 that – thanks to a fluke – Allied forces first began crossing the Rhine (at Remagen, just north of Koblenz where the photographs in this book were selected; although the original bridge has been replaced, and most of the German towns in the vicinity have been practically rebuilt after suffering insuperable damage, this sleepy village still makes a historically interesting afternoon out).

Three days later the Allies had four divisions across the river, and shortly afterwards Anglo-American armoured forces were sweeping all before them in the long-delayed drive on Berlin, while the Russians converged in even greater strength from the east. The critically important industrial area of the Ruhr – still a depressing region to visit – was encircled, trapping two Panzer armies, and ancient German cities began to collapse like windfalls: Heidelberg and Hamburg among them. The Anglo-Americans linked hands with the Russians over the River Elbe and, although there was sporadic fighting in Berlin and points south in Czechoslovakia, Bavaria and Austria, the campaign and the war were essentially over.

Throughout, German Panzer troops had fought with superlative courage and tenacity both despite and because of the orders of a madman but, inevitably, God was on the side of the 'big battalions'.

About the Photographs

The photographs in this book have been selected with care from the Bundesarchiv, Koblenz (the approximate German equivalent of the US National Archives or the British Public Records Office). Particular attention has been devoted to choosing photographs which will be fresh to the majority of readers, although it is inevitable that one or two may be familiar. Other than this, the author's prime concern has been to choose good-quality photographs which illustrate the type of detail that enthusiasts and modellers require. In certain instances quality has, to a degree, been sacrificed in order to include a particularly interesting photograph. For the most part, however, the quality speaks for itself.

The Bundesarchiv files hold some one million black and white negatives of Wehrmacht and Luftwaffe subjects, including 150,000 on the Kriegsmarine, some 20,000 glass negatives from the inter-war period and several hundred colour photographs. Sheer numbers is one of the problems which makes the compilation of a book such as this difficult. Other difficulties include the fact that, in the vast majority of cases, the negatives have not been printed so the researcher is forced to look through box after box of 35 mm contact strips – some 250 boxes containing an average of over 5,000 pictures each, plus folders containing a further 115,000 contact prints of the Waffen-SS; moreover, cataloguing and indexing the negatives is neither an easy nor a short task, with the result that, at the present time, Luftwaffe and Wehrmacht subjects as well as entirely separate theatres of operations are intermingled in the same files.

There is a simple explanation for this confusion. The Bundesarchiv photographs were taken by war correspondents attached to German military units, and the negatives were originally stored in the Reich Propaganda Ministry in Berlin. Towards the close of World War 2, all the photographs – then numbering some $3\frac{1}{2}$ million – were ordered to be destroyed. One man in the Ministry, a Herr Evers, realised that they should be preserved for posterity and, acting entirely unofficially and on his own initiative, commandeered the first available suitable transport – two refrigerated fish trucks – loaded the negatives into them, and set out for safety. Unfortunately, one of the trucks disappeared en route and, to this day, nobody knows what happened to it. The remainder were captured by the Americans and shipped to Washington, where they remained for 20 years before the majority were returned to the government of West Germany. A large number, however, still reside in Washington. Thus the Bundesarchiv files are incomplete, with infuriating gaps for any researcher. Specifically, they end in the autumn of 1944, after Arnhem, and thus record none of the drama of the closing months of the war.

The photographs are currently housed in a modern office block in Koblenz, overlooking the River Mosel. The priceless negatives are stored in the basement, and there are strict security checks on anyone seeking admission to the Bildarchiv (Photo Archive). Regretably, and the author has been asked to stress this point, the archives are *only open to bona fide authors and publishers, and prints can only be supplied for reproduction in a book or magazine.* They CANNOT be supplied to private collectors or enthusiasts for personal use, so *please* – don't write to the Bundesarchiv or the publishers of this book asking for copy prints, because they cannot be provided. The well-equipped photo laboratory at the Bundesarchiv is only capable of handling some 80 to 100 prints per day because each is printed individually under strictly controlled conditions – another reason for the fine quality of the photographs but also a contributory factor in the above legislation.

Right Interesting shot of PzKpfw IVHs of the 2nd Panzer division in a French farmyard. They carry the alternative 'trident' marking instead of the more usual inverted 'Y' divisional insignia. The condition of the trees suggest that this photo was taken in the autumn of 1944 (298/1761/8a).

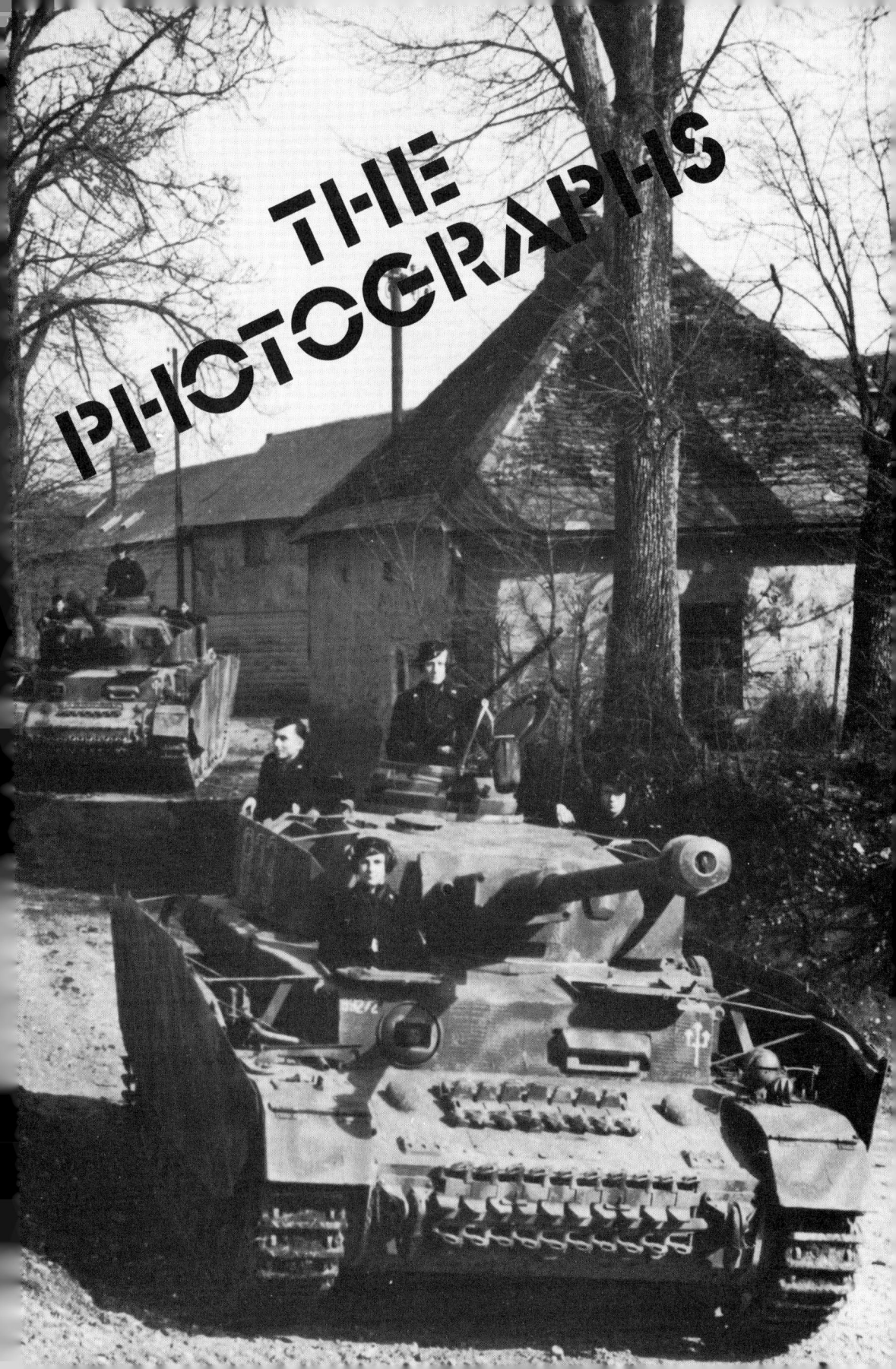

THE PHOTOGRAPHS

Above left Before D-Day. Field Marshal Erwin Rommel with other German officers during an inspection of the Atlantic Wall defences (298/1758/19).

Left As news of the Allied landings spread, units were rushed from all over Europe to try to contain the beach-head. Here, a StuG III with long-barrelled 7·5 cm gun and *Saukopf* mantlet moves through a Belgian town (297/1733/5).

Above Rail transport was widely used to move armoured equipment quickly, which was one reason the Allied air forces concentrated so much of their effort on wrecking track and depots. These vehicles are StuG IIIs again (288/1770/20).

Right A PzKpfw IVH with L/48 7·5 cm gun and apron armour. The Germans made extensive use of foliage to break up the outline of their vehicles (493/3356/7).

Background photograph *Festung Europa*. A Pak 40 anti-tank gun emplacement on the French coast, with massive concrete fortification behind it. Exposed positions like this suffered heavy casualties from Allied aircraft and naval gunfire on D-Day (297/1735/14).

Inset photographs From the flatness of the countryside, these two shots of PzKpfw IVHs were probably taken in Holland. Colour scheme appears to be the standard dark yellow oversprayed with irregular streaks of dark green and red-brown or grey. Note the unusual outline stencil form of turret numbering (288/1759/25 and 288/1760/28a).

Above left Tiger I of an SS division in a French village. The camouflage is similar to that seen on the previous PzKpfw IVs but the tank has orthodox white outline turret numbering (299/1804/4).

Left Trio of Tiger Is on a winding French road. Note SS mottle camouflage jacket worn by the commander of the foreground vehicle with black peaked field cap (299/1804/15).

Above The same type of camouflaged jacket being worn with the SS officers' 'old-style' field cap by this Unterscharführer (469/3471/17).

Above right Unterscharführer from a Panzer regiment of the 1st SS Panzer Division Leibstandarte 'Adolf Hitler'. The sleeve eagle and shoulder strap insignia are very clearly shown on his black Panzer jacket, here unusually worn buttoned up at the throat. He also wears the SS-pattern camouflaged field cap and sports a colourful neckscarf (297/1725/33).

Right Convoy in a French lane. The motorcycle sidecar appears to carry a letter 'M' on a white patch on its rear (494/3392/10a).

Above left An Army PzKpfw V Panther in a Normandy wood (296/1651/20).

Above right PzKpfw IV in the Normandy bocage (588/2276/4).

Below 'Fed up with this game, I wanna go home.' Disgruntled MG 34 gunner hitching a ride on a Panther. Note gaiters worn with the short ankle boots (301/1955/29).

Keeping a watchful eye for Allied aircraft are the crew of a 20 mm Flak 38 (**above**) and Flakpanzer IV Wirbelwind (**below**). The crew of the former are wearing reversible camouflage smocks and three of them have string netting on their helmets into which foliage could be placed for camouflage. The Wirbelwind is so liberally covered in hay that it appears to have been through a whirlwind! (495/3430/9 and 496/3455/9).

Above Fallschirmjägers and their prey – a Sherman. Note the officer's camouflage smock. Foreground vehicle is an NSU Kettenrad tracked motorcycle while behind it is a White scout car (497/3533/18).

Below Close-up of the knocked-out Sherman (497/3533/22).

Above German soldiers examining a British Cromwell tank (494/3376/37a).

Below Another sorry-looking Cromwell which appears to have been thoroughly looted – even the Besa machine-gun is missing (494/3376/19a).

Above and above right The Germans made extensive use of captured Allied vehicles with prominent crosses painted on them for rapid identification by their own forces. These two shots show an M4A2 Sherman with M1A2 76 mm gun. Can anyone explain the box-like structure on the front? (496/3454/15 and 496/3455/15).

Left Another Sherman captured by Fallschirmjäger – note camouflage smocks and helmet carried by foreground figure. The significance of the name on the turret stowage box is unknown (494/3376/30a).

Right Heavily laden M8 Greyhound armoured car impressed into German service. Its basic olive drab camouflage appears to have been over-painted in typical German fashion in a lighter colour, possibly yellow (301/1955/13).

Above The ubiquitous Jeep was as popular with the Germans as with the Americans and British. The Bren gun also seems to have been valued! (493/3358/3a).

Below M10 Hellcat in German service. The unit insignia clearly visible on the hull rear is a mystery. It is *not* 20th Panzer Division since this unit served exclusively in Russia, so what is it? (494/3383/39a).

Right A Tiger I of the 1st SS Panzer Division Leibstandarte 'Adolf Hitler' on the move towards the front (299/1805/20).

Above German infantry in the bocage. The two men on the right are wearing Wehrmacht-pattern reversible smocks and helmet covers (494/3383/30a).

Left As well as captured Allied vehicles, the Germans also used a variety of obsolete or converted French equipment, as shown in this and the following pictures. Here, Hotchkiss H-39s (redesignated PzKpfw 39-H 735 (f) in German service) advance through a village. Note that the original dome-shaped cupolas have been replaced by split hatches as was normal German practice (300/1858/31a).

Above A German hybrid, the 7·5 cm Pak 40 L/48 auf Gw Lr S (f) – in other words, a Pak 40 anti-tank gun mounted on the chassis of the French Lorraine tractor. 184 such vehicles were made and used in Europe up to the end of 1944 (297/1701/33).

Right Less potent was the 4·7 cm Pak (t) auf Gw Renault R 35 (f) shown here – a Czech 4·7 cm anti-tank gun mounted on obsolete French Renault R 35 chassis, and also used in North-West Europe. This and the preceding two photos were probably taken in early spring 1944 (297/1724/12a).

Left and above The French Hotchkiss H-39 chassis provided the basis for these vehicles mounting Pak 40 anti-tank guns, designated 7·5 cm Pak 40 L/48 auf Gw Hotchkiss (f). Basic camouflage appears to be sand and brown or green (493/3359/31 and 493/3365/20).

Left, right and above right Although they look virtually identical to the SPGs shown in the top two photographs, these are actually 10·5 cm Panzerhaubitze 18 auf Sf 39 H (f)s, in other words, H-39 chassis mounting 10·5 cm le FH 18 howitzers: the gun barrel is the give-away (493/3356/4, 493/3359/34 and 493/3365/4).

Above StuG III preceded by a Panther, probably in the south of France. Note elaborate camouflage pattern on the StuG's side skirts (588/2300/9).

Left Far more potent than the StuG III was the Jagdpanzer IV (SdKfz 162). This is a late production version with the StuK 42 L/70 gun and carries the insignia of the 116th Panzer Division above the tactical device denoting a 3rd Company vehicle (496/3464a/6).

Above right A close-up of another vehicle from the same unit clearly showing the zimmerit anti-magnetic mine paste finish and the use of foliage to break up the vehicle's silhouette (496/3464a/12).

Right Another picture from the same sequence showing the Jagdpanzer IV's skirt armour and even more dense camouflage! (496/3464a/5).

Above The same vehicle being overtaken by another from the same unit. It is interesting that, out of these four photos, only one Jagdpanzer carries divisional or tactical markings (496/3464/14).

Above right and right StuG III crewed by Fallschirmjäger personnel. Note the way the shirtsleeved commander is wearing his headphones (588/2281/27a and 28a).

Below Panzer-Grenadier's view from a StuG III on the Western Front. The commander's shoulder insignia is not clear but appears to be the 'GD' initials of Panzer-Grenadier Division 'Grossdeutschland', which would make the StuG a 26th Panzer Regiment vehicle (678/8200/31).

Above left A troop of StuG IIIs hide from Allied aerial observation in an empty factory building. The crews are all wearing the standard field-grey uniform for SPG personnel (297/1733/2).

Left Knocked-out PzKpfw 38(t). This Czech light tank was still being used by German recce units as late as 1944 (680/8282/15).

Above The 2nd Panzer Division insignia shown earlier is very clearly marked on this PzKpfw IVH (298/1759/34).

Right A break in the fighting for the crew of a PzKpfw IV. Note overalls worn by standing figure and the signalman badge on the arm of the seated man (680/8282/32).

Background photograph The havoc caused by Allied aerial bombardment. This *was* St Lo! (494/3398/27).

Also widely used in North-West Europe were the Marder III Ausf M **(inset right)**, an SPG on the PzKpfw 38(t) chassis carrying a 7·5 cm Pak 40; and the Hetzer **(inset left)** with a 7·5 cm L/70 weapon. This vehicle also belongs to the 'Grossdeutschland' Division. The Marder appears to have been photographed in Belgium or Holland (297/1729/23 and 679/8200/37).

Directing the battle. **Above** Field Marshal von Rundstedt (left) with 'Panzer' Meyer, Witt and Sepp Dietrich. **Below** SS General Paul Hausser flanked by senior Luftwaffe officers (297/1739/16a and 586/243/7a).

Above Line-up of PzKpfw IVs of the SS Panzer Division 'Hitler Jugend' (297/1740/19a).

Below 'Hitler Jugend' personnel relax while watched dourly by a pair of French villagers (297/1726/17).

Left Good shot of a motorcycle despatch rider showing the special rubberised coat. The bike is a Zundapp. Photo probably taken autumn 1944 (297/1743/21).

Right 'Hitler Jugend' PzKpfw IVH on the move (297/1725/32).

Below and following two pages These five photos all illustrate one vehicle of the SS Panzer Division 'Hitler Jugend' and will be ideal for modellers wishing to create an individual vehicle. The turret number, 615, appears to be red, outlined white. The girl's name 'Wilma' is in white in two positions on the commander's cupola, while the name 'Paula' appears over the driver's visor. Note battered condition of the trackguards and side skirts. Basic colour scheme appears to be dark yellow oversprayed with green and brown. Note that several personnel are wearing black leather U-boat clothing, a peculiarity singular to the 'Hitler Jugend' Division (297/1722/23, 24, 26, 28 and 297/1725/37).

Above left Close-up of a guitar-strumming Unterscharführer of the same unit. His rank distinctions are very clear but note absence of the SS eagle from his left sleeve, and non-regulation roll-neck sweater (297/1726/3).

Left Close-up of the turret of another 'Hitler Jugend' PzKpfw IVH. The texture of the zimmerit finish is very clear. Turret number in this case *appears* to be black rather than red, and white (297/1725/9).

Above Fallschirmjäger motorcyclist driving through the ruins of another French town (586/2208/3a).

Right Tiger I after an attack by Allied rocket-firing aircraft! Part of the turret can be seen up-ended in the foreground (494/3397/4a).

These pages, overleaf top and title page One of the commonest sights in Normandy during the fateful summer of 1944 – PzKpfw V Panthers, liberally camouflaged with local foliage, and carrying Panzer-Grenadiers into battle. These photographs should also be especially useful to modellers (301/1954/6 and 301/1955/17, 18, 20, 22 and 32).

Below left, this page and following three pages Huge numbers of German tanks were destroyed, mainly from the air, during the fighting around Villers Bocage, as can be seen from these photographs of Leibstandarte-SS 'Adolf Hitler' PzKpfw IVs and Tiger Is. Note divisional insignia and tactical device for a heavy tank company – a lozenge containing an 'S' (494/3376/7a to 14a).

Above Although this picture is said to have been taken in Normandy, it seems more likely that this unfortunate old PzKpfw IV with short-barrelled 7·5 cm gun was destroyed on a test range – see the meaning of 'Versuchs' in the glossary. Serial numbers are, in any case, very rare on AFVs on active service (680/8282/16).

Below Much the same probably applies to this battered Marder III (680/8282/13).

Above PzKpfw IVHs and staff cars of a Panzer regiment HQ advance along a typical French tree-lined road (493/3354/2a).

Below StuG III of an SS unit (note mottle camouflage uniform jacket worn by commander) moves past the Hotel de la Poste in a French town (497/3506a/32a).

Opposite German use of foliage to break up the silhouettes of their vehicles is abundantly clear in these two shots of StuG IIIs on the Western Front (497/3506/22a and 24a).

OVERLEAF Background photograph Marder III Ausf Ms move past a half-timbered French farmhouse. Despite the infantryman in the foreground, it seems unlikely anyone is firing back or surely the foreground vehicle's commander would not be exposing himself in this way? (298/1768/6). **Inset** German infantry hitch a lift on another Marder III. This and the background photograph were probably taken during manoeuvres (298/1768/25).

Above left Even ack-ack crews have to eat some time! Luftwaffe Flak 88 detachment enjoying a lunch break in a French field (496/3468a/24).

Left 20 mm Flak 38 mounted on an unidentifiable vehicle (496/3457a/20).

Panzer commanders. **Above** Army Hauptfeldwebel (note rank stripes on arms) wearing the *Pour le Mérite*. **Above right** Army Leutnant wearing the 'old-style' field cap and Iron Cross 1st Class. **Right** SS Sturmbannführer of the 'Hitler Jugend' Division wearing the Knight's Cross. **Overleaf** The highest-scoring German tank commander of the war, Leibstandarte 'Adolf Hitler' Obersturmführer Michael Wittman poses on the turret of his Tiger I. His decorations include the Knight's Cross and Iron Cross 1st Class. Note the more rounded lapels on his SS Panzer jacket which differentiated it from that worn by Army tank crewmen (298/1761/33a, 298/1759/26, 297/1739/22a and 299/1802/8).

Above PzKpfw IVH. The white interior paint used on German AFVs can clearly be seen on the open turret side hatch door. Note chevrons on the Gefreiter's left arm. The device on the tank's front mudguard could, possibly, be that of the 21st Panzer Division (493/3355/24).

Right Michael Wittman (on left) with the crew of his own Tiger and another officer from the Leibstandarte-SS 'Adolf Hitler'. They are wearing the special mottle-camouflaged SS version of the standard Panzer jacket and trousers, with a variety of grey and black shirts (299/1802/2).

These four photos well illustrate the exceptionally clean lines and well-sloped armour of the Jagdpanther, a self-propelled 8·8 cm gun on the Panther tank chassis which is widely acknowledged to have been the most formidable tank destroyer of the entire war. These particular pictures appear to have been taken during a demonstration since no unit or tactical markings are evident, nor do the vehicles even carry machine-guns in their bow sockets! (679/8200/10, 22 and 24 and 721/396/14).

Infantry anti-tank weapons. **Above left** Infantryman in Army-pattern camouflage smock and heavily foliaged helmet with a Panzerfaust. **Left** Racketenpanzerbüchse 54, an 8·8 cm 'bazooka'; note goggles worn to protect the eyes from the flash (586/2219/31 and 494/3396/24).

Above German infantry demonstrate a captured bazooka for the camera. Note MP 40 magazine pouches, camouflaged helmet cover and Iron Crosses 1st and 2nd Class worn by the soldier on the left (494/3396/6).

Right Another view of an RPzB 54 being used by a Fallschirmjäger (587/2263/29).

Opposite Two views of 15 cm Panzerwerfer 42 'Maultier' half-tracks carrying appropriate tactical signs (apparently in grey on dark yellow background) and the number plates 'WH-1409023' and 'WH-1409052'. This vehicle was a lightly armoured version of the famous Opel Maultier half-track, using Carden-Lloyd suspension, and carrying ten 15 cm Nebelwerfer tubes. Stencilled letter 'X's above the numerals '8' and '9' respectively are visible on the sides, the number '8' being repeated larger on the hull side of the former vehicle but being inexplicably replaced by the letter 'C' on the latter (300/1858/27a and 300/1859/4).

Right Tiger I of an unidentified Army unit on the Western Front. The crew are wearing one-piece overalls. Note that the man pointing across the gun barrel wears his peaked field cap back to front! (301/1951/26).

Below right Another view of the same vehicle. The man in the foreground is a Gefreiter (301/1951/27).

OVERLEAF

Background photograph If someone pointed one at me, I'd surrender! German infantry demonstrate their portable flamethrowers (296/1670/13).

Left inset An LSSAH Tiger in a French town. Note two-piece mottle camouflage overalls (493/3362/19).

Right inset PzKpfw IVH, autumn 1944. Note repetition of turret number '831' on side skirt (298/1760/20a).

Left Roadside rest for a Panther. Note spare wheel on turret side. The two foreground figures wear Oberfeldwebel shoulder strap insignia (301/1960/38).

Below left General Hasso von Manteuffel (left) with Oberst von Bronsart in September 1944. Although he had relinquished command of the 'Grossdeutschland' Division at the beginning of this month, Manteuffel still wears its cuff title on the sleeve of his leather greatcoat (301/1961/8a).

Above right The Tiger II, or Königstiger, was the most powerful tank in the world in 1944 and an ideal defensive weapon. Here, a very 'clean' vehicle is having camouflage paint sprayed over its basic colour scheme (721/398/21a).

Right Field Marshal von Rundstedt inspecting an anti-aircraft position. The gun, interestingly, is a captured Russian Degtyarev 7·62 mm machine-gun with 47-round drum magazine, the implication being that the unit under inspection is probably a second line or reserve formation (298/1774/18).

OVERLEAF

Good detail views for modellers of a 7·5 cm Pak 40. Note the wires strung across the front of the shield to take camouflage and the fact that, even this late in the war (autumn 1944) one of the men's helmets still has a Wehrmacht eagle decal on its side (296/1688/28a and 297/1723/24).

Top and above Two views of Tiger IIs well hidden from aerial observation in a wood. The two British prisoners with the wheelbarrow look cheerful enough – at least for them the war is over! (721/359/37 and 721/363/5).

Right Luftwaffe anti-aircraft gunner anxiously scans the skies for prowling Allied aircraft. From the shape of the shield, the gun could well be a 20 mm Gebirgsflak 38, a standard Flak 38 on a lightened carriage for use by mountain troops, of which 180 were built (497/3509/31).

Above left Well-camouflaged Panzer-Grenadiers hitch a lift on the turret of a Panther (301/1955/24).

Left PzKpfw IVH undergoing running repairs. The support rails can clearly be seen in the absence of the side skirts (493/3355/23).

Above Disabled Tiger I. Look at the barrel! (494/3376/5a).

Below and overleaf top Tiger IIs in Germany before being sent to the front (721/397/27 and 29).

Below Luftwaffe motorcyclist outside a farmhouse. An MP 40 sub-machine-gun can just be seen alongside the briefcase in the sidecar (495/3432/36).

Right Flak 88 being readied for action. Its Luftwaffe crew wear a variety of uniforms, including white and grey denim overalls and the stylish Fliegerbluse (495/3432/21).

OVERLEAF Background photograph Army Panzer crewmen on their best behaviour, probably about to be decorated. The Feldwebel third from left wears a marksman's lanyard (296/1651/5). **Inset** PzKpfw IVH without side skirts but with turret apron (493/3365/27).

Left MG 42 in its heavy machine-gun guise manned by a Fallschirmjäger trooper in camouflaged smock (587/2263/35).

Below left Men of a Luftwaffe field unit confer over their maps. The officer in the centre is an Oberleutnant (494/3397/24).

Right Infantry in camouflage smocks and helmet covers confer with a Leutnant from a self-propelled gun unit wearing the field grey version of the Panzer jacket (495/3435/38a).

Below An officer points out directions to a group of Fallschirmjäger, probably from a recce unit since five of them are wearing motorcycle goggles (586/2208/33a).

Above Modellers should look especially hard at this shot of a Panther turning a corner – note how its weight has shifted on to the braking track (497/3513/2).

Left Repairing the track on a StuG III (298/1771/9).

Above right Pak 38 in a defensive position overlooking a river (497/3518/31).

Right German infantry advance past an abandoned Airborne 6 pdr anti-tank gun (494/3383/28a).

Left Good close-up of the breech end of a Flak 88 (496/3491/36).

Right The epic battle for Arnhem – a Marder III moves along a lane past the wing of a Horsa glider (493/3364/7).

Below Captured British paratroopers in Arnhem with a StuG III. The German soldier in the centre wears SS-pattern mottle camouflage (497/3527/19a).

OVERLEAF

Background photograph Tiger Is on the move through Holland (299/1804/7).

Inset StuG III in Oosterbeek (497/3529/6).

This page Panthers move through a Dutch town. One of the signposts clearly reads 'Peiper' but the others are indecipherable (300/1876/2a and 4a).

Right SS Schwimmwagen and Tiger I in a Dutch town. The lettering on the arm of the SS driver on the right of the picture is unfortunately illegible, but under a glass could just possibly be 'Der Führer' – ie, one of the regiments in the 2nd SS Panzer Division 'Das Reich' (299/1804/6).

Above Marder III with German infantry during the long retreat (297/1746/5).

Below The end in sight. The ice on the puddle indicates that this picture was probably taken in early winter 1944, one of the few such late pictures in the Bundesarchiv collection (301/1955/26).

1. German Order of Battle, June 6 1944 – Panzer Divisions

Panzer Lehr Division (based near Orleans): Panzer Regiment 130, Panzer-Grenadier Regiments 901 and 902, Artillery Regiment 130, Recce Battalion 130, Anti-tank Battalion 130, Signal Battalion 130, Flak Abteilung 311 plus supporting services.

2nd Panzer Division (based near Amiens): Panzer Regiment 3, Panzer-Grenadier regiments 2 and 304, Artillery Regiment 74, Recce Battalion 2, Anti-tank Battalion 38, Signal Battalion 38, Flak Abteilung 273 plus supporting services.

9th Panzer Division (based near Arles): Panzer Regiment 33, Panzer-Grenadier Regiments 10 and 11, Artillery Regiment 102, Recce Battalion 9, Anti-tank Battalion 50, Signal Battalion 82, Flak Abteilung 287 plus supporting services.

11th Panzer Division (based near Bordeaux): Panzer Regiment 15, Panzer-Grenadier Regiments 110 and 111, Artillery Regiment 119, Recce Battalion 11, Anti-tank Battalion 61, Signal Battalion 341, Flak Abteilung 277 plus supporting services.

21st Panzer Division (based near Caen): Panzer Regiment 22, Panzer-Grenadier Regiments 125 and 192, Artillery Regiment 155, Recce Battalion 21, Anti-tank Battalion 200, Signal Battalion 200, Flak Abteilung 305, Sturmgeschütze Battalion 200 (added later) plus supporting services.

116th Panzer Division (based near Rouen): Panzer Regiment 16, Panzer-Grenadier Regiments 60 and 156, Artillery Regiment 146, Recce Battalion 116, Anti-tank Battalion 228, Signal Battalion 228, Flak Abteilung 281, Sturmgeschütze Battalion 936 plus supporting services.

19th Panzer Division (based near Nijmegen): Panzer Regiment 27, Panzer-Grenadier Regiments 73 and 74, Artillery Regiment 19, Recce Battalion 19, Anti-tank Battalion 19, Signal Battalion 19, Flak Abteilung 19 plus supporting services.

1st SS Panzer Division Leibstandarte 'Adolf Hitler' (based at Beverloo): SS Panzer Regiment 1, SS Panzer-Grenadier Regiments 1 and 2, SS Artillery Regiment 1, SS Recce Battalion 1, SS Anti-tank Battalion 1, SS Signal Battalion 1, SS Flak Abteilung 1, SS Sturmgeschütze Battalion 1 plus supporting services.

2nd SS Panzer Division 'Das Reich' (based near Toulouse): SS Panzer Regiment 2, SS Panzer-Grenadier Regiments 3 'Deutschland' and 4 'Der Führer', SS Artillery Regiment 2, SS Recce Battalion 2, SS Anti-tank Battalion 2, SS signal Battalion 2, SS Flak Abteilung 2 plus supporting services.

12th SS Panzer Division 'Hitler Jugend' (based near Lisieux): SS Panzer Division 12, SS Panzer-Grenadier Regiments 25 and 26, all other formations as above, numbered '12'.

2. Select glossary of German military terms

Abteilung: Unit, battery, battalion.
Aufklärungs: Reconnaissance.
Abwehr: Intelligence.
Armee: Army.
Artillerie: Artillery.
Ausbildungs: Training.
Bataillon: Battalion.
Batterie: Battery.
Bau: Construction.
Begleit: Escort.
Beobachtungs: Survey, observation.
Befehlshaber: Commander.
Brücken: Bridge (eg, *Brücken-Baubataillon* = bridge-building unit).
Chef: Chief.
Eisenbahn: Railway (eg, *Eisenbahn-Panzer-Zug* = armoured train).
Ersatz: Training, depot, replacement.
Fahrkolonne: Horse-drawn supply column.
Fallschirm: Parachute.
Feld: Field.
Feldgendarmerie: Military police.
Feldhaubitze: Field howitzer.

Feldlazarett: Field hospital.
Feldwerkstatt: Field workshop.
Feldzeug: Ordnance.
Fernsprech: Telephone.
Festungs: Fortress.
Flak: Anti-aircraft (eg, *Flakpanzer* = anti-aircraft tank).
Flammenwerfer: Flamethrower.
Funk: Wireless, radio (eg, *Funkwagen* = radio car).
Gebirgs: Mountain.
Geschütze: Gun.
Granatwerfer: Mortar, grenade thrower.
Grenadier: Grenadier, rifleman.
Grenz: Frontier.
Haubitze: Howitzer.
Heeres: Army.
Infanterie: Infantry.
Jagdpanzer: Tank destroyer.
Jäger: Literally, 'hunter'; in military terms, a light infantryman (eg, *Fallschirmjäger* = paratrooper, *Gebirgsjäger* = mountain trooper).
Kannonier: Gunner.
Kanone: Cannon, gun.
Kavallerie: Cavalry.
Kommandant: Commandant, commander.
Kommando: HQ, command.
Kompanie: Company.
Kraftfahrzeug: M/T repair.
Kraftwagen: Truck, lorry.
Krankenkraftwagen: Ambulance.
Kriegsmarine: Navy.
Lehr: Demonstration.
leichte: Light (eg, leFH = *leichte Feldhaubitze* = light field howitzer).
Luftwaffe: Air Force.
Maschinen-Gewehr: Machine-gun (eg, MG 42).
Maschinen-Pistole: Machine pistol, sub-machine-gun (eg, MP 40).
Mörser: Mortar.
Munitions: Ammunition.
Nachrichten: Signals.
Nachschub: Supply.
Nebelwerfer: Smoke projector.
Offizier; Officer.
Panzer: Armour.
Panzerbefehlswagen: Command tank.
Panzerbeobachtungswagen: OP tank.
Panzerkampfwagen (PzKpfw): Tank.
Panzerjäger: Tank hunter.
Panzerspähwagen: Armoured car.
Pferde: Horse.
Pioneer: Engineer.
Sanitäts: Medical.
Scheinwerfer: Searchlight.
Schützenpanzerwagen: Armoured personnel carrier.
Schutzstaffel: SS.
schwere: Heavy (eg, sFH = *schwere Feldhaubitze* = heavy field howitzer).
Sonder: Special (eg, SdKfz = *Sonderkraftfahrzeug* = special purposes motor vehicle, as applied to all forms of military transport, wheeled or tracked).
Stab: Staff.
Sturmboot: Assault boat.
Sturmgeschütze: Assault gun.
Truppe: Troop, detachment.
Versuchs: Experimental.
Wach: Guard.
Waffen: Weapon.
Waffen-SS: Literally, 'weapon-SS' – the fighting branch of the SS.
Waffenträger: Weapons carrier.
Wehrmacht: Armed forces.
Werfer: Projector.
Zug: Platoon, section.
Zugkraftwagen: Tractor.

Other titles in the same series

No 1 Panzers in the desert
by Bruce Quarrie

No 2 German bombers over England
by Bryan Philpott

No 3 Waffen-SS in Russia
by Bruce Quarrie

No 4 Fighters defending the Reich
by Bryan Philpott

No 6 German fighters over the Med
by Bryan Philpott

In preparation

No 7 German paratroops in the Med
by Bruce Quarrie

No 8 German bombers over Russia
by Bryan Philpott

No 9 Panzers in Russia
by Bruce Quarrie

No 10 German fighters over England
by Bryan Philpott

Plus many more!